D0100036

Get Started With
STEM

Wings, Paws, Scales, and Claws

Let's Investigate Animal Bodies

by Ruth Owen

Ruby Tuesday Books

Published in 2017 by Ruby Tuesday Books Ltd.

Copyright © 2017 Ruby Tuesday Books Ltd.

Editor: Mark J. Sachner
Designer: Emma Randall
Consultant: Judy Wearing, PhD, BEd
Production: John Lingham

Photo credits:
Alamy: 16; FLPA: 8, 9, 10, 11 (top), 14 (bottom), 15 (top), 20, 24–25, 31 (bottom left); Nature Picture Library: 29 (top), 30 (top); Ruby Tuesday Books: 11 (bottom); Shutterstock: Cover, 1, 2–3, 4–5, 6–7, 12–13, 14 (top), 15 (bottom), 17, 18–19, 21, 22–23, 26–27, 28, 29 (bottom), 30 (bottom), 31 (top), 31 (bottom right).

Library of Congress Control Number: 2016918448

ISBN 978-1-911341-47-5

Printed and published in the United States of America

For further information including rights and permissions requests, please contact our Customer Service Department at 877-337-8577.

Contents

Awesome Body Bits 4

Let's Get Sorting! 6

Meet the Mammals 8

Made for the Cold 10

Beautiful Birds 12

Lots of Changes 14

Meet the Reptiles 16

Incredible Insects 18

Sensational Spiders 20

Fantastic Fish 22

What Is a Bat? 24

What's for Dinner? 26

Open Wide 28

Claws and Paws 30

Glossary, Index 32

Words shown in **bold** in the text are explained in the glossary.

The download button shows there are free worksheets or other resources available. Go to:

www.rubytuesdaybooks.com/getstarted

Awesome Body Bits

Eyes, ears, legs, paws—this book is all about animals and their bodies.

People are animals, too. Human and animal bodies have a lot of the same parts, but they don't look the same.

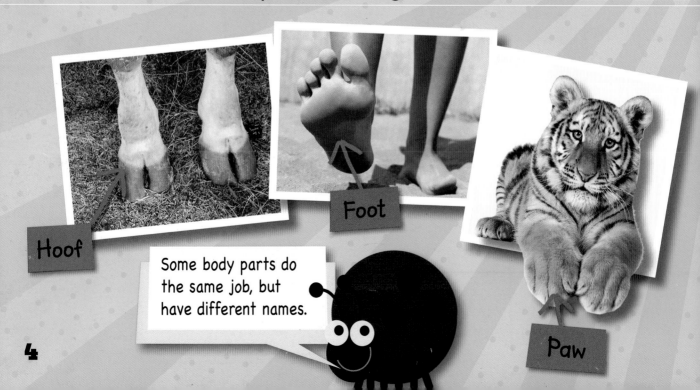

Hoof

Foot

Paw

Some body parts do the same job, but have different names.

Ear

Eye

In what ways is a giraffe's body similar to a human's? How is it different?

Mouth

Neck

Back

Shoulder

Tail

Does a giraffe have body parts that you don't have?

Belly

Do you have body parts that a giraffe doesn't have?

Leg

Knee

Hoof

Let's Get Sorting!

Scientists often sort animals into groups. This makes it easier to talk about how they are alike and different.

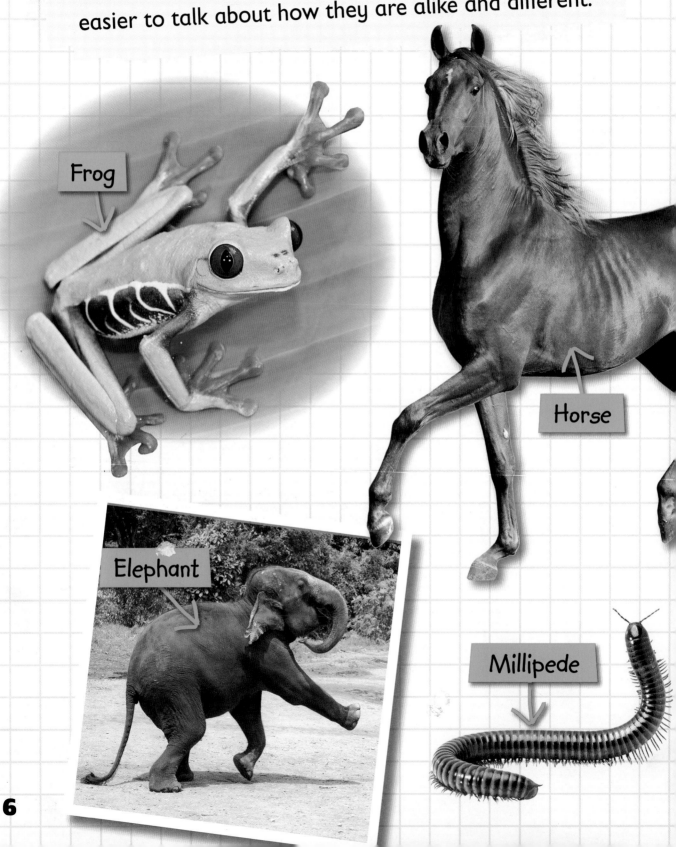

Frog

Horse

Elephant

Millipede

Butterfly

Snake

Parrot

Be a Scientist!

Look at the bodies of the animals on these pages.

Can you see a way to sort the animals into two groups?
Is there more than one way to sort them?

(There are some ideas at the bottom of the page.)

Crab

Fish

Answer: Here are three ways to sort the animals: wings and no wings; tail and no tail; legs and no legs.

7

Meet the Mammals

Scientists sort animals into groups. Some groups are **mammals**, birds, **amphibians**, **reptiles**, insects, spiders, and fish. So what is a mammal?

A mammal is an animal with fur or hair on its body.

Mountain gorilla

Some mammals, such as whales and dolphins, live in the sea.

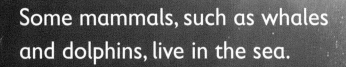

Blue whale

These animals don't look hairy, but they do have some tough hairs, or bristles, on their bodies.

A blue whale is the largest animal on Earth. It can weigh as much as 30 elephants.

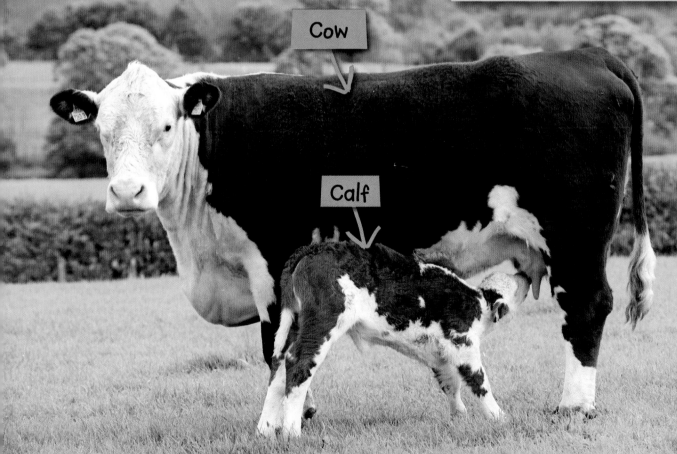

Cow

Calf

All mammal mothers produce milk to feed to their babies.

Made for the Cold

A polar bear is a large mammal. Its body is adapted for life in the freezing-cold Arctic.

To stay warm, a polar bear has a long, thick top layer of fur and a short, woolly undercoat.

Polar bear

It also has a thick layer of fat under its fur.

Polar bear paw

A polar bear's paw is the size of a dinner plate. It has fur and bumpy pads on the bottom for gripping the slippery ice.

Be a Scientist!

When polar bears hunt for seals, they often swim in the icy ocean.

How do you think a bear's fat helps it in the water?

Gather your equipment:
- A sandwich bag
- Vegetable shortening, such as Crisco
- A mixing bowl of water
- Ice cubes
- A rubber band

1. Put the fat into the bag. Add the ice cubes to the bowl of water.

2. Put your left hand into the icy water for about 30 seconds.

How does your left hand feel?

3. Now push your right hand into the bag of fat and secure it with a rubber band. Put this hand into the water for 30 seconds.

How does your right hand feel?

How do you think a bear's fat helps it?

(The answer is at the bottom of the page.)

Answer: The hand inside the bag of fat stayed warmer than the other hand. That's because the fat protected the hand from the cold. A polar bear's fat protects its body from the icy sea.

Beautiful Birds

All birds have wings and feathers. Most birds use their wings to fly, but some birds, such as penguins and ostriches, can't fly.

Robin

Toucan

Can you observe some other ways that birds are the same?
(There are some ideas below.)

Barn owl

Duck

Penguin

Answer: All birds have two legs and a beak.

Birds have differently shaped beaks because they eat different foods.

Look at the four pictures.

Can you match the beaks to these descriptions?

1) A beak for catching worms and insects.

2) A beak for grabbing fish and frogs from ponds.

3) A beak for tearing meat.

4) A beak for cracking hard nuts and seeds.

(The answers are at the bottom of the page.)

Heron

Parrot

Robin

Owl

A hummingbird has a long beak for drinking nectar from flowers. As it hovers in front of a flower, it beats its wings 50 times each second.

Hummingbird

Lots of Changes

Frogs, toads, newts, and salamanders are amphibians. These animals begin their lives in water.

Frog

Salamander

Toad

As adults, they spend time in water and on land.

A newt hatches from an egg as a tiny **larva**.

When it's two months old, it grows front legs.

Larva

Leg

The larva gets bigger, and its back legs grow.

Gills

Young amphibians breathe underwater through body parts called **gills**. Once they are adults, they breathe in air through their skin and with lungs.

When it is about five months old, a young newt is ready to live on land.

Adult newt

Meet the Reptiles

Reptiles are animals with skin that is covered with tough **scales**.

Old skin

As it grows, a snake's scaly skin gets too tight. It also gets damaged.

Scales

Grass snake

Several times a year, a snake sheds its skin.

Beneath the old skin, a new skin has grown.

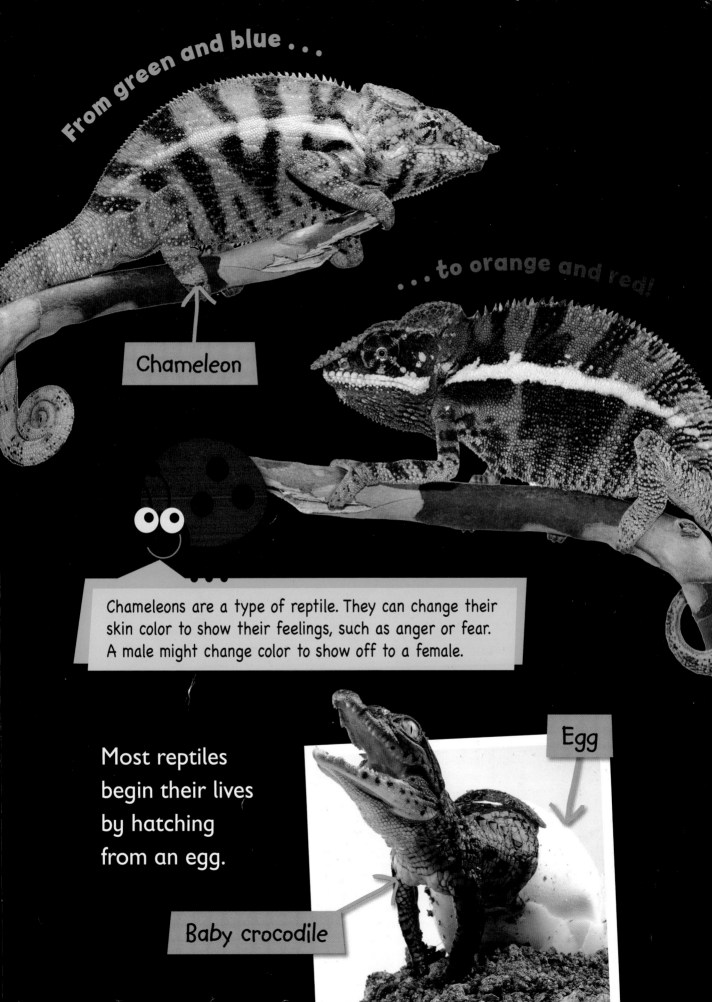

From green and blue . . .

. . . to orange and red!

Chameleon

Chameleons are a type of reptile. They can change their skin color to show their feelings, such as anger or fear. A male might change color to show off to a female.

Egg

Most reptiles begin their lives by hatching from an egg.

Baby crocodile

Incredible Insects

Insects come in different shapes and sizes, but they all have three pairs of legs.

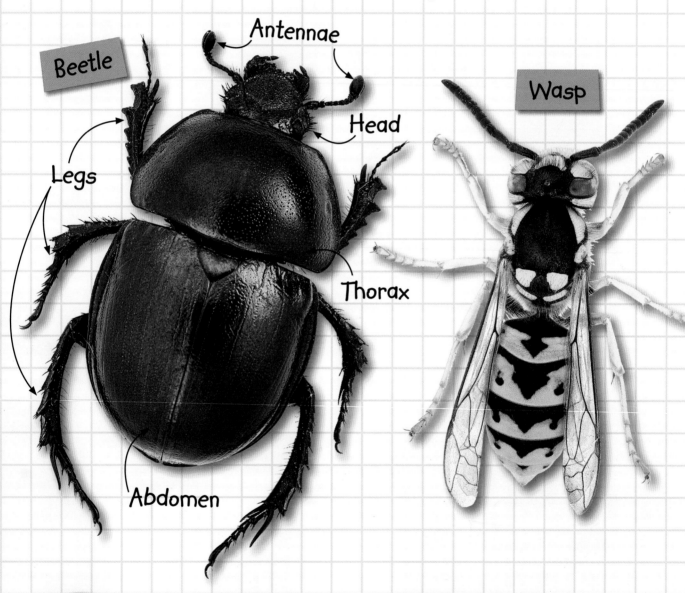

Beetle

Antennae

Head

Legs

Thorax

Abdomen

Wasp

Insects have a body in three parts, called the head, thorax, and abdomen.

Many insects also have wings.

All insects have a pair of antennae. Insects use their antennae to do different things, such as touching, smelling, or detecting sounds.

Antennae

Buff tip moth

When a buff tip moth closes its wings, it looks like a piece of broken twig.

This helps it hide from birds and other **predators** that might eat it.

19

Sensational Spiders

Spiders are animals with eight legs and a body in two parts.

Goliath birdeater spider

The biggest spider in the world is the Goliath birdeater.

Two body parts

The legs of this spider can measure 12 inches (30 cm) across.

A Goliath birdeater doesn't usually eat birds. It actually feeds on small ground animals, such as worms and frogs.

Most spiders have eight eyes.

A jumping spider uses its eyes to help it spot and jump on **prey**.

Eyes

Jumping spider

Fly

Let's Test It!

Carefully observe the body of each little animal shown here.

Is it a spider or an insect?

(The answers are below.)

A

B

C

D

Answers: **Spiders:** A) Banded garden spider C) Ladybird spider **Insects:** B) Earwig D) Shield bug

Fantastic Fish

Fish are animals that spend all their lives in water. They live in ponds, streams, rivers, lakes, and oceans.

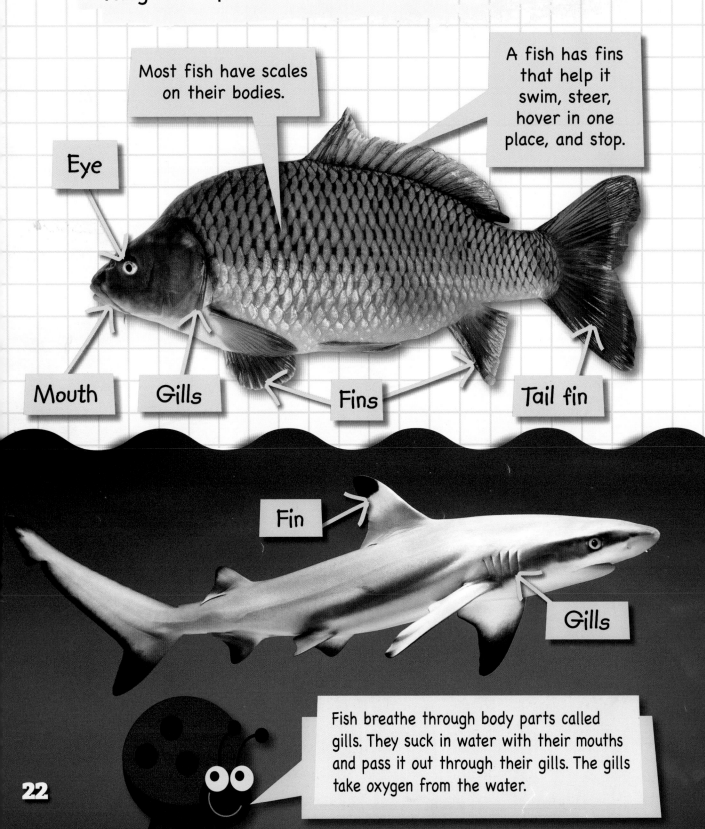

Most fish have scales on their bodies.

A fish has fins that help it swim, steer, hover in one place, and stop.

Eye

Mouth

Gills

Fins

Tail fin

Fin

Gills

Fish breathe through body parts called gills. They suck in water with their mouths and pass it out through their gills. The gills take oxygen from the water.

The great white shark is the world's largest predatory fish.

It can grow to be 20 feet (6 m) long.

Great white shark

Sea lion

A great white shark hunts for ocean animals such as seals and sea lions.

A life-size great white shark tooth

What Is a Bat?

Bats are animals with furry bodies and wings.

Many types of bats are predators that hunt for flying insects at night.

Bat

A single bat might catch 3,000 insects in one night!

Let's Talk

Look at the bat's body. Which of these animal groups do you think a bat belongs to?

**Reptiles Birds
Mammals Insects**

(The answer is at the bottom of the page.)

Answer: Bats are mammals. They are the only type of mammal that can fly.

What's for Dinner?

Another way to sort animals into groups is by the type of food they eat.

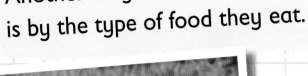
Rhino

Guinea pig

Animals that only eat plants are called herbivores.

Sheep

Snail

Eagle

Animals that only eat other animals are called carnivores.

Lion

Ladybug

Frog

Some animals eat plants and meat. These animals are omnivores.

Panda

Crow

Fox

Chicken

Be a Scientist!

Try sorting animals into herbivores, carnivores, and omnivores.

You can do this by drawing a Venn diagram in a notebook.

Write the animal's name in the correct section of the diagram.

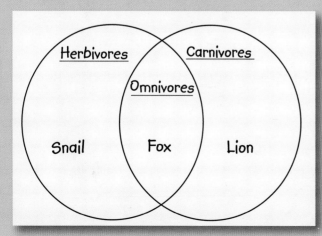

Herbivores — Carnivores

Omnivores

Snail   Fox   Lion

Add the animals on these pages to your diagram.

Look back through the book to find other animals to add.

If you have a pet, what do you feed it? Is it a herbivore, carnivore, or omnivore?

Add your pet to the diagram.

Where does your name go on the diagram?

Open Wide

We can often tell what food an animal eats by looking at its teeth.

Canine tooth

A carnivore has four long, sharp teeth called canine teeth for tearing at meat.

Herbivores have large incisor teeth for slicing through plants.

They also have big molars for grinding plants.

Horse skull

Incisors

Molars

Snakes have long, thin teeth called **fangs**.

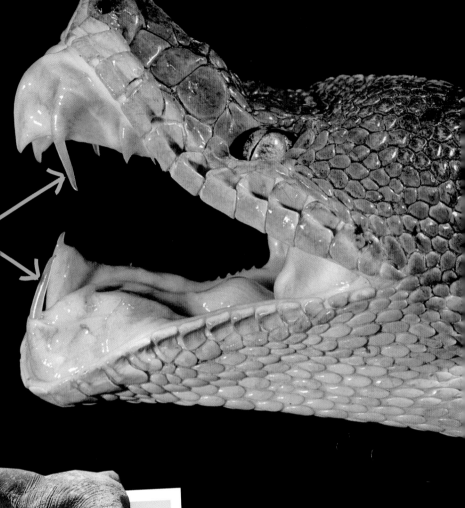

Fangs

They inject **venom** into their prey with their fangs.

An elephant's tusks are actually super long front teeth.

Tusk

Elephants use their tusks to dig for water. They also dig for roots and use their tusks to strip tasty bark from trees.

Claws and Paws

Many animals have long claws, but they don't all use them in the same way.

All members of the cat family have sharp claws for grabbing and holding prey.

Lynx

Osprey

An osprey uses its sharp claws, or talons, to grab and lift fish from water.

Sloths are slow-moving animals that live in trees.

Sloth →

They use their long claws to climb and hang upside-down from branches.

Badger

Sett entrance

Badger paw

Badgers use their claws to dig underground homes called setts. They also dig for worms, which are their favorite food.

Glossary

amphibian (am-FIB-ee-uhn)
An animal, such as a frog, toad, or newt, that begins its life in water and lives on land as an adult.

fangs (FANGZ)
Long, sharp teeth that animals, such as snakes and spiders, use to inject venom into prey.

gills (GILZ)
Body parts that some animals use for breathing underwater. Fish and young amphibians have gills.

larva (LAR-vuh)
A young insect or amphibian.

mammal (MAM-uhl)
An animal with hair, fur, or wool. Mammals give birth to their babies and feed them milk.

predator (PRED-uh-tur)
An animal that hunts and eats other animals.

prey (PRAY)
An animal that is hunted by other animals for food.

reptile (REP-tile)
An animal, such as a snake, lizard, tortoise, turtle, crocodile, or alligator, that has scales and lives on land.

scales (SKAYLZ)
Small, tough, overlapping plates, or sections, that cover the skin of reptiles and some fish.

venom (VEN-uhm)
Poison that is injected into a person or animal through a bite or sting.

Index

A
amphibians 6, 8, 14–15, 26

B
birds 7, 8, 12–13, 19, 20, 25, 26–27, 30

F
fish 7, 8, 13, 22–23, 30

I
insects 7, 8, 13, 18–19, 21, 24–25, 26

M
mammals 4–5, 6, 8–9, 10–11, 24–25, 26–27, 28–29, 30–31

R
reptiles 7, 8, 16–17, 25, 29

S
spiders 8, 20–21